The Military Wedding

by

Vanessa L. Baldwin

Bloomington, IN  Milton Keynes, UK

authorHOUSE®

AuthorHouse™
1663 Liberty Drive, Suite 200
Bloomington, IN 47403
www. authorhouse. com
Phone: 1-800-839-8640

AuthorHouse™ UK Ltd.
500 Avebury Boulevard
Central Milton Keynes, MK9 2BE
www. authorhouse. co. uk
Phone: 08001974150

First published by AuthorHouse 1/2/2008

Printed in the United States of America
Bloomington, Indiana
This book is printed on acid-free paper.

ISBN: 978-1-4343-1795-7 (sc)

Library of Congress Control Number: 2007905640

CONTENTS

DEDICATION

In memory of my mother, Mrs. Margarie Spencer (a former
military spouse) and my friend and mentor, Dr. Cortez H. Martin
In honor of my stepfather, Mr. Samuel Spencer (a veteran), my
aunt, Mrs. Georgia Stainback, my godmother, Mrs. Evelyn Moody,
family and friends, too numerous to list, who supported me as I
pursued my military career.

ACKNOWLEDGEMENTS

I will never forget one of my Wedding Coordination Certificate Program students, Mrs. Cheryle Bracewell, who pleaded with me to publish this book. Having been a military bride, she knew there was a need for a book like this and felt that I should be the one to write it.

I want to thank all of the military brides who complained to me about how little information was available to plan a military wedding. They gave me the idea and encouraged me. You were my inspiration.

I want to thank my Northern Virginia Community College Woodbridge Campus Wedding Coordination Certificate Program students and Program Developer, Sparkle Raymond, who helped keep my dream alive.

Thank you to my cousins, Jackie LaBoard and Veronica Benson; my long time friends, Lydia Mathis, Cheryl Malone, and Renee Frazier; my Officer Training School roommate and long time friend, Dianna Batchelor. Thank you to my soror and long time friend, Wanda Pemberton and my soror, high school choir and driving buddy, Victoria Thomas Jones, who never lost touch with me during my military career. I thank Rev. Marvin T. Glenn, Rev. Dr. Barbara Y. Glenn and my Agape Sisters, Annette Griffis, the Rev. Judy Johnson-Joyner, Gayle McMahan, Vivian Pace and Carole Rose, who saw me through the good and bad times during the early military retirement years. Thank you for your laughter, tears, and especially the prayers, words of encouragement and unconditional love that kept me going. Thank you to Rev. Barbara Taylor, who introduced me to the military weddings.

Thank you to Arnold and Cheryl Leverett, of Saint Marys, Georgia and Johnny and Regina Harris, of San Angelo, Texas, who I met in the military. They encouraged me to pursue my dreams and always made me feel like a special part of their families.

To my First AME Church of Alexandria, Virginia family, I love you!

Vanessa L. Baldwin, CWC

INTRODUCTION

As a wedding consultant, who specializes in military weddings, I hear brides, who are trying to plan military weddings, lament about the lack of information available about military weddings. Brides are marrying later and are better educated. Even if they are hiring a wedding consultant to plan a military wedding, the brides still want to know as much as possible. Most wedding planning and etiquette books briefly address military weddings, but not to the satisfaction of most military brides.

There are situations that face the bride or groom marrying a military person that a civilian couple doesn't always have to face. In addition to embarking on a new journey as a married couple, the military wedding is the beginning of a whole new way of life and culture. A severe case of culture shock may manifest once the new military spouse arrives at the spouse's duty location. Welcome to the brave new world of military jargon, acronyms, ID cards, wives' clubs, customs and courtesies, personnel reassignments, deployments and on and on. Becoming a military spouse is also an exciting adventure--full of new and exotic places, as well as challenges that will test the foundation of your marriage. Or, it will strengthen your partnership as husband and wife, bound by the fondest memories of shared experiences, adventures and challenges conquered. It's enough to make a strong person weak in the knees. It's not a life for the faint of heart.

So, this book, *The Military Wedding*, has been written to make the experience less harrowing and more enjoyable. This book is mainly written for the civilian bride marrying a military groom, but I will try not to overlook the civilian groom marrying a military woman and the military bride and groom. A few paragraphs, as found in most books, won't answer your questions. Consider this your military wedding planning manual or special operating instruction to supplement your main wedding planning guide.

Last, but not least, keep your sense of humor. Have a beautiful, memorable military wedding and marriage!

CHAPTER 1
Engagement

Congratulations on your engagement! You've decided to have a military wedding. You ask yourself, "What do I do now?" Here's a good place to start:

Arrange to meet your fiance's family. If you are marrying someone in the military, your parents may not live near to where you and your fiance live. Arrange a meeting well in advance of the wedding date, since you may have to travel a considerable distance to meet your future in-laws.

Also, consider when your parents will have a chance to meet. Arrange for your parents to meet each other well in advance of the wedding date instead of at the rehearsal, which is the day before your wedding. During one of these meetings, be sure to discuss who will pay for what—just like any other wedding.

Select a date. When you select a date, be prepared to be flexible, especially if you are planning your ceremony in a military chapel or your reception in the officers' or enlisted clubs. So, have back-up dates in mind—maybe even a plan for an alternate venue.

Some chapels are in great demand for weddings. Once you are engaged and decide you want your wedding at a military chapel, call the chapel to find out the eligibility criteria, application requirements and available dates. There may be a priority list to reserve the chapel based on military duty status. If one of you is on active duty, you may be able to reserve the chapel up to one year in advance. Reservists and retirees may have some restrictions on how far in advance they may reserve the chapel.

Save the Date Cards and Letters. Save the date cards and letters are wonderful if your wedding date is at least six months or more away and you expect a lot of guests from out of town. Save the date information can be in the form of a personal letter, newsletter, computer printed or professional printed announcements. The purpose is to give your out-of-town family and friends enough advance notice about your wedding to plan time off from work, purchase reduced fare airline tickets, make hotel reservations and plan for trip expenses. If you decide to use a newsletter for your save the date information, you could also include information about any special arrangements (or discounts) you have made with hotels and airlines, activities scheduled for the weekend, directions, reservation registration forms, etc. To get the most benefit from sending save the date cards and letters, send them at least six months before the wedding date.

When deciding what format you want to use, consider the ambiance you want to create--formal, festive or informative. This is like a sneak preview. It's the first indication your guests will have about your wedding.

Examples

> *Please save the date of*
> *Saturday, the twenty-fourth of November*
> *(Thanksgiving weekend)*
> *for the wedding of*
> *Jane Susan Smith*
> *and*
> *John Edward Jones*
> *Invitation to* follow

Please Save the Date!
We will be getting married
on Saturday, November 24, 2007
in Arlington, Virginia

Invitation and details to follow
Jane Smith and John Jones

Chapter 2

Planning Your Wedding and Military Wedding Customs

The Military Chapel

Traditionally, military weddings are held at military chapels, although this is not a requirement. For couples overseas, this makes getting married easier and more like home![1]

As with civilian churches, a military chapel must be reserved as soon as possible. (Service Academy Chapels are often reserved a year in advance.) All chapel weddings are religious in nature; consult the chaplain once you reserve the chapel. He or she may wish to arrange counseling several months prior to the wedding. If he or she is officiating at the ceremony, this is also an ideal time for the chaplain to get acquainted with the couple before the ceremony. Couples preparing for a wedding in a military chapel should consider these questions:

- Are there any restrictions when using the chapel? (i.e. pew bows, flowers, aisle runners, rental equipment, etc.)

- Do you want your civilian clergyperson to officiate or assist the chaplain?

- Will it be necessary to arrange for an organist? Can you use musicians other than the chapel organist? Do you want a soloist?

- Does the chapel furnish any decorations, flowers, or candles? Are there vases or flower stands available for use?

- Do you want to light a unity candle?

- When would the rehearsal be convenient for the chaplain or clergyperson, and when is the chapel available for the rehearsal? Some chapels do not require the chaplain to attend the rehearsal. If the chaplain or other clergyperson is not present for the rehearsal, the wedding coordinator directs the rehearsal.

- Is a sabre arch planned? Does the chapel have the sabres available? If not, can the sabres be borrowed from another chapel, a ceremonial unit or the local ROTC (Reserve Officers Training Corps) unit? (Navy officers and Marines usually have their own swords.) Does the chaplain prefer that the arch be held indoors or outdoors? (Usually, weapons, even ceremonial weapons, are not allowed in the sanctuary.)

- Which rooms are available for the bride and bridesmaids, and for the groom and best man, before the wedding? Are the rooms large enough for the bride to dress at the chapel, or should the entire wedding party dress before coming to the chapel?

There is no charge for the use of a military chapel or for the services of a military chaplain; however, a donation to the chapel fund is traditional. A check made out to the chapel fund, not to the chaplain, should be given to the chaplain or chapel assistant sometime prior to the wedding. Call the chapel to find out the information to complete the check payable information. No set amount is expected. As a guideline, the suggested donation should range from $25-250.

If a civilian clergyperson assists, he should receive a fee for services rendered, usually presented in a sealed envelope by the best man prior to the ceremony. The groom traditionally pays this expense.

If you and your fiancé are not regular church goers and do not want to have your wedding in the chapel, there are other alternatives, such as military museums, historical homes or any other place the bride and groom desire. The uniforms, not the location, make it a military wedding.

Wedding Coordinator

A wedding coordinator should be hired to assist the couple in planning the details of their wedding and directing the rehearsal, ceremony and reception. Military chapels may require couples to use a wedding coordinator and may provide a list of people who offer this helpful service. The coordinator can answer the questions addressed above which pertain to the chapel and provide information about local vendors, including caterers and florists. Such details as opening, closing and cleaning the chapel are also the responsibility of the wedding coordinator.[2] Before asking a family friend to act as your coordinator, check with the chapel to determine if you are required to use one of the chapel's recommended or approved coordinators.

Wedding Photographs and Videos

The chaplain and/or wedding coordinator should be consulted for guidance on any special photography or videography requests, restrictions or suggestions. Some chaplains, as well as civilian clergy, prohibit all photography or restrict flash photography during the ceremony because the wedding ceremony is a sacred ceremony just like a worship service. Certainly, everyone concerned will want the photographer and videographer to remain as unobtrusive as possible. Also, the photographer and videographer should check with the wedding coordinator or chapel staff to find out if there are any photo or video restrictions when shooting outside of the chapel.

Arch of Sabres

Such memorable traditions as the sabre arch may be added to accentuate the fact that the groom, or the bride, is a commissioned military officer. Usually, the Army spells the word "saber." While the Air Force usually uses the British spelling, "sabre." The Navy and Marines use swords; therefore, they refer to the arch as the "Sword Arch."[3]

Six to eight ushers or ceremonial team members in uniform create the arch. The ushers may be from different branches of service and, thus, in different uniforms. If there are not enough ushers in uniform, other guests in the appropriate uniform may be asked to assist the ushers in performing this tradition.

The arch should be performed outside of the chapel. Weapons are not allowed in most chapels. Although the sabres and swords are ceremonial, they are still weapons. The sabres or swords may be left in a side room or the church foyer until after the wedding ceremony.

Wherever the arch is formed, the military detail is formed in pairs, drawing their sabres on command and holding them together over the walkway for the newlyweds to walk under the arch. Traditionally, the sabre bearers rotate their sabres so that the cutting edge is up, thus, forming a more-true arch.

The arch is usually formed on the outdoor steps. The bridal party usually stands on both sides of the door, or, at the end of the column, with the guests along the steps and sidewalk. If weather does not permit, consider having the arch performed as the newlyweds enter the reception after the social hour.

After the recessional, the wedding party and immediate family should be secluded in a side room or alcove and may return to the sanctuary to take formal photographs while the guests exit the sanctuary. The arch is not performed when the wedding party exits during the recessional because no one will be outside to observe the tradition. If the weather is too cold or you want your guests to immediately proceed to the reception, the arch may be performed after the guests exit the chapel. Then, the wedding party returns to the church for photographs. Ask your coordinator to make an announcement to your guests to proceed to the reception rather than waiting for the wedding party to depart.

When the photo session is complete, the family and wedding party, without the bride and groom, exit the church. Then, the sabre or sword team marches out to form the arch. The wedding coordinator or best man should let the bride and groom know when the arch ceremony is ready. The wedding coordinator or maid of honor assists the bride with her train, if necessary. It is recommended that the train be bustled or detached before exiting the chapel. If sabres are not available or cannot be borrowed, the uniformed ushers may still form a double line for the couple to pass through before entering their limousine.

As the bride and groom appear in the doorway, the sabre or sword team leader announces: "Ladies and gentlemen, may I present Lieutenant and Mrs. Jones!" and they enter the arch. Only the bride and groom pass under the formed arch. The last sabre bearers may then lower sabres, blocking the bridal couple from exiting and may announce, "A kiss to pass!" The couple kisses and, naturally, the wedding guests applaud. During some arch ceremonies, I have seen each pair of sabre bearers block the bride and groom's passage and demand "A kiss to pass!" A Marine Corps tradition, adopted by the other services, the last sabre bearer "taps" the bride with his sabre and offers the fond greeting, "Welcome to the Air Force (or, Army, Navy or Marine Corps), Ma'am." Because sabres are oiled, be careful of the bride's gown. Since procedures change over time, always check the service directives to ensure you have the most current information on how to perform the sabre or sword arch.

Music

If you use the chapel's organist, the organist receives a fee for the ceremony. This service is above and beyond the chapel organist's normal duty. Some chapels may have a list of musicians approved to play the chapel's organ. Expect to pay an additional sum for the rehearsal, and more if he or she rehearses with and accompanies a soloist. A soloist receives compensation as well. Neither the organist or soloist is really necessary for the rehearsal, but arrangements need to be made with them well in advance regarding the music desired. The bride's family traditionally pays these fees prior to the wedding.

Also, you may not be limited to using the chapel's organist. You may want to add a trumpeter. Or, you may want a string quartet, harpist, pianist or some other instrument played during your ceremony.

Military Ceremony Ideas

To add more military ruffles and flourishes to your wedding, here are some suggestions:

- Arrange for herald trumpets to play a fanfare to announce the bride's entrance or as the newlyweds exit from the chapel. It's especially nice if you are going to depart in a horse drawn carriage.

- Include service hymns in the ceremony (for example, playing "Eternal Father, Strong to Save" as the bride and groom light the unity candle)

- Use the service song for the recessional (for example, the Air Force Song for Air Force weddings)

- Have the sabre arch team members (without swords/sabres) line the aisle like sentries when the bride and her father walk down the aisle. The team marches out after the bride and her father pass through the sentry column.

- Hire a sabre arch team

- Have the national flag, service flag and unit flag posted behind the chaplain or officiant's position during the ceremony. The flags are already present in most chapels.[4]

- Include any significant historical information about the chapel in the program.

- Include your at home address on the back of the program, especially if you will be moving shortly after the wedding. Family and friends can stay in touch or continue to send wedding gifts after your move.

- Hire a HumVee limousine.

- Take wedding photos in front of military or national monuments or scenic views on the installation. Be sure to find out if special permission must be granted.

- If you can't schedule a military chapel, consider another site of military significance.

The military wedding ceremony should be sincerely and tastefully conducted and not insulting to the military members present.

Chapter 3

Academy Weddings

There is a special category of military wedding, those held in military academy chapels. Even if you are not getting married in an academy chapel, this chapter may have some useful information and insights for all brides who are getting married in a military chapel.

We have all heard at one time about the weddings that take place in academy chapels at the end of Commencement or Graduation Week, where the wedding date has been reserved years in advance. The picturesque scene of a dashing groom in uniform and a beautiful bride, newly married, leaving the chapel through an arch of sabres or swords. It's like something you see in a movie or on television. Granted, it's a bit dated, especially since academy graduates are, now, both male and female. However, weddings are held in academy chapels throughout the year -- not just at the end of the academic year. These weddings require just as much, if not more planning.

Application submission

Sometimes weddings held in academy chapels are scheduled more than a year in advance. All of the academies require you to submit an application for permission to hold your wedding in the chapel, if you are eligible. Applications for some academies may be found online at the academy's official website.

Eligibility criteria

Eligibility to use a service academy chapel is as varied as the number of academies. The only eligibility criteria the academies have in common is that academy alumni are eligible to use the chapel of their respective academy. Some academies extend the criteria to graduates of other service academies and active duty military members and their dependents with a valid identification card, who are assigned to the service academy. To find out the most current categories of eligible users, you must contact the chaplain for the academy chapel where you want to hold your wedding.

United States Air Force Academy
2348 Sijan Drive, Suite 100
USAFA CO 80840
(719) 333-2636

United States Military Academy
West Point NY 10996
(845) 938-2784

United States Naval Academy
101 Cooper Road
Annapolis MD 21402
(410) 293-1105

United States Coast Guard Academy
15 Mohegan Avenue
New London CT 06320
(860) 701-6729

Unites States Merchant Marine Academy
Mariners' Memorial Chapel
Kings Point NY 11024
(516) 773-5305

The other requirements and restrictions for using academy chapels are similar to using other military chapels. If not provided, when you receive your blank application form, be sure to ask for a list of policies, requirements, restrictions and prohibitions.

Officiants

Most academies require a military chaplain on staff at the academy's chapel to officiate. However, they may make exceptions for civilian clergy with the approval of the senior staff chaplain.

Music

Most academies have fabulous and very sophisticated organs. As a result, they are very restrictive about who can play the chapel's organ. It is usually limited to the chapel's organist on staff. Expect to pay a fee. This service is above and beyond the chapel organist's normal duty and is not covered by your tax dollars.

Wedding Coordinators

Shakespeare wrote, "A rose by any other name would smell as sweet." There are lots of names used to describe wedding coordinators--some sweet, some not so sweet. Whatever you call them, they are still wedding coordinators. All of the academy chapels require a chapel approved wedding coordinator, wedding facilitator, chapel assistant or chapel wedding assistant to be present for the rehearsal and the wedding ceremony. Their duties may include, but are not limited to, supervising the use of the chapel. In other words, the wedding coordinator ensures you comply with the rules and regulations for using the chapel including keeping you and your wedding party on schedule. There are still some strict time limits for your rehearsal and ceremony. At some academies, you must hire the wedding coordinator. The coordinator may be a paid staff member at other academies. Check with the academy chapel staff.

So, you've decided to get married in an academy chapel. It does not free you from thinking through the same concerns you would have at another military chapel or civilian church. Be sure to ask your academy wedding coordinator questions. The other chapters in this book give you a great place to start. You do not want any last minute surprises. And, you do not want to hear your own voice ringing in your ears saying, "But, I thought..." Ask the questions.

Don't frustrate yourself and your wedding coordinator on your wedding day by something you thought, heard or thought you heard, but didn't take the time to clarify. It's better to ask permission before your wedding day, than to beg forgiveness on your wedding day and not receive it. As in any chapel, your chaplain, chapel approved wedding coordinator or chapel assistant has the authority to stop your wedding because of a rule violation.

It may be *your* special day, but avoid disaster by following the rules. All weddings are beautiful even the ones plagued by problems, disappointments, crises and disasters. The only truly terrible wedding is the one where the couple leaves the ceremony still unmarried. Don't let this happen to you because you insist that it is your day and fail to comply with the rules for using the facility whether your wedding is set to take place in an academy chapel, military chapel or other location.

Chapter 4

Invitations and Announcements

The key to selecting invitations for a military wedding is to make sure the invitations are chosen with good taste and are a reflection of the style of the bride and groom. A few etiquette and protocol rules to observe when preparing your invitation wording:

1. A father-of-the-bride who is a retired officer uses his military rank. He does not note on the invitation that he is retired, unless he is a widower and issuing the invitation in his name alone.

2. If the groom or father-of-the-bride is retired military, and issues the invitation in his name only, that status is noted on the invitations in this manner:

   Lieutenant Colonel John Edward Jones
   United States Air Force, Retired

3. Both first and second lieutenants of the Army are designated simply as Lieutenant, but those in the Air Force or Marines use their complete title:

   John Edward Jones
   First Lieutenant, United States Marine Corps

4. For noncommissioned officers and enlisted men, rank is usually omitted. Their full name is written on one line, with the branch of service underneath:

   John Edward Jones
   United States Army

Special Invitations

You should send invitations to the bride's parents and the groom's parents as well as all of the bridal party, as keepsakes. When a military member gets married, it is courtesy to send an invitation to the commander and spouse.

It is also courteous to send an invitation to the chapel organist, or musician, and the chaplain, or person performing the ceremony, and their spouses. These invitations should be mailed the same as for other invited guests.

Announcements

Wedding announcements may be used in addition to wedding invitations. Announcements may be sent to friends and relatives who live too far away to attend the wedding and to local friends and relatives when the wedding and reception list is too small to accommodate everyone. Announcements carry no obligation for a gift; however, courtesy requires at least a warm note of congratulation. Usually wedding announcements are mailed the day after the wedding, never before. The announcement resembles the wedding invitation in every way except wording.[3] Check your wedding etiquette book for the appropriate wording.

Invitations for Children

Children and babies should not be taken to a wedding or reception, unless their names are included on the invitation. Those who are invited and attend should be well behaved. Just in case, your guests are not as etiquette or protocol savvy as you, check with your wedding coordinator to determine if there is a "cry room."

Chapter 5

Wedding Attire

It is not the location of either the wedding or reception that creates a military wedding. The military uniforms make the wedding a military wedding. It's not only the uniforms, but also the uniformity that's the highlight of a military wedding. The uniforms chosen determine the style and formality of the wedding.

During a military wedding, all military members of the wedding party should wear the same uniform. For example, if the groom is wearing a mess dress uniform, his best man, groomsmen and ushers, who are military, wear the mess dress uniform. If the best man, groomsmen and ushers are of different branches of service, they wear their service's version of the uniform that the groom is wearing. It's the same as being in military formation. Everyone is dressed the same. It creates a striking appearance when all of the military members are uniformly dressed. If there is a female attendant in the wedding party, who will be in uniform, the same applies.

If the bride is in the military, she may choose to wear civilian attire or her uniform. If she selects a uniform and the groom is also in the military, he wears the same type of uniform as the bride. Other military members of the wedding party (male or female) dressed in uniform should wear the same type of uniform, or if in a different service, a uniform of comparable formality.

Female military members of the wedding party may wear uniforms or traditional civilian clothing, whichever the bride and groom prefer. However, the female military members of the wedding party may only participate in the sabre or sword arch if they are in uniform.

Anyone in the bridal party not in the military should wear the appropriate civilian attire for the formality of the wedding.

Military guests may choose to wear their uniforms (same type as the wedding party), or civilian clothing. The bride and groom frequently prefer military members to wear their uniforms for a military wedding; so, if you are a guest, you may want to ask their preference.

Again, always check your service directives for current information on the appropriate uniform for the formality and the time of day of the wedding

Attire for the Bride

Very Formal Evening	Dress with a long train. Veil (often same length as train) to complement dress. Long sleeves or gloves to cover arms. Shoes to match dress. Full bouquet or flower-trimmed bible or prayer book.
Very Formal Daytime	Same as very formal evening, but shorter train is also appropriate.
Formal Evening	Long dress with a chapel, sweep, or detachable train. Veil of a length to complement dress. Accessories the same as those for a very formal wedding.
Formal Daytime	Same as formal evening or a shorter dress that may have a detachable train. Hat or veil of a length to complement dress.
Semiformal Evening	Long or shorter dress, white or pastel. Train is optional. Veil from floor-length to flyaway. Same accessories as a formal wedding, but a simpler bouquet is used.
Semiformal Daytime	Stylish dress, white or pastel color, short veil. Small bouquet or flower-trimmed prayer book.
Informal	Suit or stylish dress (white is optional). Veil or hat, gloves, shoes and bag. Small bouquet.

Attire for the Military Bride
(For active duty, retired and reserve service members)

Very Formal Evening	*Officer and Enlisted*: Mess Dress uniform (Optional: Appropriate civilian attire.)
Very Formal Daytime	*Officer and Enlisted*: Mess Dress uniform (Optional: Appropriate civilian attire.)
Formal Evening	*Officer*: Mess Dress uniform *Enlisted*: Mess Dress uniform or semi-formal service dress uniform (Optional: Appropriate civilian attire.)
Formal Daytime	*Officer*: Mess Dress uniform *Enlisted*: Mess Dress uniform or semi-formal service dress uniform (Optional: Appropriate civilian attire.)
Semiformal Evening	Mess Dress Uniform or semi-formal service dress uniform (Optional: Appropriate civilian attire.)
Semiformal Daytime	Semi-formal service dress uniform or service dress uniform (Optional: Appropriate civilian attire.)
Informal	Service dress uniform (Optional: Appropriate civilian attire.)

Attire for Bridesmaids

Very Formal Evening	Long dresses, gloves to complement sleeve length. Any style bouquet, shoes to match color scheme. Hair ornaments or flowers.
Very Formal Daytime	Same overall style as very formal evening, but dresses are often less elaborate.
Formal Evening	Similar to very formal, but dresses are sometimes short. Gloves are optional.)
Formal Daytime	Dresses either long or short, but not too elaborate. Matching or color- coordinated accessories, including bouquets.
Semiformal Evening	Elaborate evening dresses. Small bouquets.
Semiformal Daytime	Suit or dress, less elaborate than semi-formal evening. Small bouquet.
Informal	Suit or stylish dress. Small bouquet.

Attire for Military Bridesmaids
(For active duty, retired and reserve service members)

Very Formal Evening	*Officer and Enlisted:* Mess Dress uniform (Optional: Appropriate civilian attire.)
Very Formal Daytime	*Officer and Enlisted:* Mess Dress uniform (Optional: Appropriate civilian attire.)
Formal Evening	*Officer:* Mess Dress uniform *Enlisted:* Mess Dress uniform or semi-formal service dress uniform (Optional: Appropriate civilian attire.)
Formal Daytime	*Officer:* Mess Dress uniform *Enlisted:* Mess Dress uniform or semi-formal service dress uniform (Optional: Appropriate civilian attire.)
Semiformal Evening	Mess Dress Uniform or semi-formal service dress uniform (Optional: Appropriate civilian attire.)
Semiformal Daytime	Semi-formal service dress uniform or service dress uniform (Optional: Appropriate civilian attire.)
Informal	Service dress uniform (Optional: Appropriate civilian attire.)

Attire for Mothers of the Bride and Groom

Very Formal Evening	Long or short evening dresses. Shoes, gloves and flowers to match color scheme.
Very Formal Daytime	Long or short dresses, not as formal as those for evening. Shoes, gloves and flowers match color scheme. Hats optional.
Formal Evening	Long or short dresses, or evening suits. Shoes, gloves and flowers.
Formal Daytime	Elegant dresses or suits. Other accessories to match. Flowers to wear. Hats optional.
Semiformal Evening	Elaborate stylish evening dresses or dinner suits with appropriate accessories. Flowers to wear.
Semiformal Daytime	Daytime luncheon suits or dresses, somewhat less elaborate than semi-formal evening. Flowers to wear.
Informal	Stylish dresses or suits. Flowers to wear.

Attire for the Mothers of the Bride and Groom (Military)
(For active duty, retired and reserve service members)

Very Formal Evening	If active duty or retired, uniform is the same as for bride and female attendants. (Optional: Appropriate civilian attire.)
Very Formal Daytime	If active duty or retired, uniform is the same as for bride and female attendants. (Optional: Appropriate civilian attire.)
Formal Evening	If active duty or retired, uniform is the same as for bride and female attendants. (Optional: Appropriate civilian attire.)
Formal Daytime	If active duty or retired, uniform is the same as for groom and male attendants. (Optional: Appropriate civilian attire.)
Semiformal Evening	Mess Dress Uniform or semi-formal service dress uniform (Optional: Appropriate civilian attire.)
Semiformal Daytime	Semi-formal service dress uniform or service dress uniform (Optional: Appropriate civilian attire.)
Informal	Service dress uniform or appropriate civilian attire (Optional: Appropriate civilian attire.)

Attire for Female Guests

Very Formal Evening	Long or short evening dresses.
Very Formal Daytime	Elegant short dresses or suits.
Formal Evening	Elegant long or short evening dresses, or suits.
Formal Daytime	Elegant daytime dresses or luncheon suits.
Semiformal Evening	Stylish evening dresses or dinner suits.
Semiformal Daytime	Stylish dresses or luncheon suits.
Informal	Stylish dresses or suits.

Attire for Groom

Very Formal Evening	Full-dress tailcoats with matching trousers, white waistcoats, white bow ties, wing-collared shirts. (Optional: Black top hats, white gloves).
Very Formal Daytime	Cutaway coats, gray striped trousers, gray waistcoats, wing-collared shirts, cufflinks and ascots or striped ties. (Optional: Top hats, spats, gray gloves.)
Formal Evening	Black tuxedos with matching trousers, tuxedo shirts, bow ties, and waistcoats or cummerbunds (Optional: White or ivory dinner jackets.)
Formal Daytime	Grey strollers, waistcoats, striped trousers, shirts, cufflinks, studs and striped ties. (Optional: Homburgs, gloves.)*
Semiformal Evening	Tuxedos or dinner jackets, dress shirts, bow ties, cufflinks, studs and vests or cummerbunds.
Semiformal Daytime	Suit, dress shirt and four-in-hand ties.
Informal	Business suits or classic blazers with coordinating trousers, dress shirt and tie.*

*Or, may choose formal suits in white or light colors for summer, darker shades for fall; dress shirts, bow ties, vests or cummerbunds.

Attire for the Military Groom
(For active duty, retired and reserve service members)

Very Formal Evening	Officer and Enlisted: Mess Dress uniform
Very Formal Daytime	Officer and Enlisted: Mess Dress uniform
Formal Evening	Officer: Mess Dress uniform Enlisted: Mess Dress uniform or semi-formal service dress uniform
Formal Daytime	Officer: Mess Dress uniform Enlisted: Mess Dress uniform or semi-formal service dress uniform
Semiformal Evening	Mess Dress Uniform or semi-formal service dress uniform
Semiformal Daytime	Semi-formal service dress uniform or service dress uniform
Informal	Service dress uniform

Attire for Male Attendants

Very Formal Evening	Full-dress tailcoats with matching trousers, white waistcoats, white bow ties, wing-collared shirts. (Optional: Black top hats, white gloves).
Very Formal Daytime	Cutaway coats, gray striped trousers, gray waistcoats, wing-collared shirts, cufflinks and ascots and ascots or striped ties. (Optional: Top hats, spats, gray gloves.)
Formal Evening	Black tuxedos with matching trousers, tuxedo shirts, bow ties, and waistcoats or cummerbunds (Optional: White or ivory dinner jackets.)
Formal Daytime	Grey strollers, waistcoats, striped trousers, shirts, cufflinks, studs and striped ties. (Optional: Homburgs, gloves.)*
Semiformal Evening	Tuxedos or dinner jackets, dress shirts, bow ties, cufflinks, studs and vests or cummerbunds.
Semiformal Daytime	Suit, dress shirt four-in-hand ties.
Informal	Business suits or classic blazers with coordinating trousers, dress shirt and tie.

Attire for Military Male Attendants

(For active duty, retired and reserve service members)

Very Formal Evening	Officer and Enlisted: Mess Dress Uniform
Very Formal Daytime	Officer and Enlisted: Mess Dress Uniform
Formal Evening	Officer: Mess Dress uniform Enlisted: Mess Dress uniform or semi-formal service dress uniform
Formal Daytime	Officer: Mess Dress uniform Enlisted: Mess Dress uniform or semi-formal service dress uniform
Semiformal Evening	Mess Dress Uniform or semi-formal service dress uniform
Semiformal Daytime	Semi-formal service dress uniform or service dress uniform
Informal	Service dress uniform

Attire for the Fathers of the Bride and Groom

Very Formal Evening	Full-dress tailcoats with matching trousers, white waistcoats, white bow ties, wing-collared shirts. (Optional: Black top hats, white gloves).
Very Formal Daytime	Cutaway coats, gray striped trousers, gray waistcoats, wing-collared shirts, cufflinks and ascots or striped ties. (Optional: Top hats, spats, gray gloves.)
Formal Evening	Black tuxedos with matching trousers, tuxedo shirts, bow ties, and waistcoats or cummerbunds (Optional: White or ivory dinner jackets.)
Formal Daytime	Grey strollers, waistcoats, striped trousers, shirts, cufflinks, studs and striped ties. (Optional: Homburgs, gloves.)*
Semiformal Evening	Tuxedos or dinner jackets, dress shirts, bow ties, cufflinks, studs and vests or cummerbunds.
Semiformal Daytime	Suit, dress shirt and four-in-hand ties.
Informal	Business suits or classic blazers with coordinating trousers, dress shirt and tie.

Attire for the Fathers of the Bride and Groom (Military)

(For active duty, retired and reserve service members)

Very Formal Evening	If active duty or retired, uniform is the same as for groom and male attendants. (Optional: Appropriate civilian attire.)
Very Formal Daytime	If active duty or retired, uniform is the same as for groom and male attendants. (Optional: Appropriate civilian attire.)
Formal Evening	If active duty or retired, uniform is the same as for groom and male attendants. (Optional: Appropriate civilian attire.)
Formal Daytime	If active duty or retired, uniform is the same as for groom and male attendants. (Optional: Appropriate civilian attire.)
Semiformal Evening	Mess Dress Uniform or semi-formal service dress uniform
Semiformal Daytime	Semi-formal service dress uniform or service dress uniform
Informal	Service dress uniform or appropriate civilian attire

Attire for Male Guests

Very Formal Evening	Black tie (tuxedos) or white tie (tails).
Very Formal Daytime	Suits.
Formal Evening	Black tie (tuxedos).
Formal Daytime	Suits.
Semiformal Evening	Black tie (optional) or suits.
Semiformal Daytime	Suits.
Informal	Suits.

Attire for Military Guests
(For active duty, retired and reserve service members)

Very Formal Evening	Mess Dress or semi- formal service dress uniform (Optional: Appropriate civilian attire.)
Very Formal Daytime	Semi-formal service dress uniform or service dress uniform (Optional: Appropriate civilian attire.)
Formal Evening	Service dress uniform (Optional: Appropriate civilian attire.)
Formal Daytime	Officers: Mess Dress uniform Enlisted: Mess Dress uniform or semi- formal service dress uniform. (Optional: Officers and enlisted may wear appropriate civilian attire.)
Semiformal Evening	Mess Dress Uniform or semi-formal service dress uniform (Optional: Appropriate civilian attire.)
Semiformal Daytime	Semi-formal service dress uniform or service dress uniform (Optional: Appropriate civilian attire.)
Informal	Service dress uniform or appropriate civilian attire. (Optional: Appropriate civilian attire.)

Chapter 6

Your Wedding Ceremony

Rehearsal

Due to time limits allowed for a rehearsal in the military chapel, the purpose of the rehearsal is not to rehearse every word of the ceremony. The purpose of the rehearsal is to practice the special seating of the parents, processional, recessional and other movement during the ceremony, including walking down the aisle at a slow, but natural pace--not a hesitation or choir step.

Rehearsal Dinner

The groom's family still is responsible to host the rehearsal dinner as detailed in most wedding planning guides and etiquette books. In addition to the wedding party, family and other special guests, the chaplain or civilian clergyperson and spouse may be included--definitely if the couple knows them well or they are good friends of the family.

Ceremony

Because of the popularity of many military chapels for military weddings, there may be specific times set for the length of time for your ceremony and photo session. Those times are firm because there may be other couples who also want to use the same chapel.

Be sure you are aware of the amount of time you are allowed for set-up and seating guests before the ceremony starts. Some chapels do not have the space for the bride to dress. But, if there is room for the bride to dress, you should arrive at the chapel, with your hair and makeup completed and dressed in everything except your wedding gown. Your honor attendant, bridesmaids, flower girl and family should arrive completely dressed. The limited time and space at the chapel does not allow for everyone to dress after they arrive at the chapel or time for dressing room clean up before the ceremony. The bride's room **must** be cleared before the ceremony in case another bridal party arrives before your ceremony is over. You wouldn't want to find a messy bride's room and neither would another bride. Also, it is not the wedding coordinator's responsibility to clean up the bride's room and the other waiting areas. The wedding coordinator is responsible for clearing the sanctuary and ensuring that you have not left any of your personal belongings. Please be respectful and considerate of your wedding coordinator and those wedding parties that come after you.

Consider the length of your ceremony. If you plan to have a Nuptial Mass, which lasts approximately one hour, you may not be able to take formal photographs in the chapel's sanctuary if you are allowed one hour for your ceremony and photographs. I would not encourage you to forego a Nuptial Mass just to have pictures taken. However, you do need to be aware of the consequences, so that you are not disappointed on your wedding day. If you recognize this, you can prepare to have group photographs taken at another scenic location. Unless the chapel or your officiant imposes strict photography restrictions, you will have photographs of your actual ceremony in the chapel's sanctuary.

Your wedding coordinator will instruct the ushers about seating guests, line up the parents and wedding party, cue the musicians when to begin the music, cue the parents and wedding party when to proceed into the sanctuary and when to exit the chapel. The wedding coordinator also directs the wedding party and family's movement after the ceremony to complete your formal photo session so you can leave the chapel as quickly as possible to begin enjoying your reception.

Ushers and Sabre Bearers

The usher's main duty is to seat the wedding guests. Plan to have at least one usher for every 50 invited guests. Groomsmen may also serve as ushers. Or, you may designate people to serve as ushers, who will not stand with the bride and groom during the ceremony. Guests should never be seated during the scripture, a reading or prayer.

The ushers should escort the guests down the outside aisles (reserving the first three pews for family and any very senior officers or commanders). Thus, the guests enter the pews from the outside aisle and proceed to as close to the center aisle as possible, giving them the best view. Seating from the outside aisles also precludes later guests from squeezing past those who are already seated.

If the groom's (or bride's) parents cannot attend the wedding, the commander and spouse may be invited to sit in their place. Otherwise, the commander and any very senior officers may be escorted to seats beside or in the pews directly behind the family.[8]

For a Catholic or Protestant ceremony, the head usher escorts the bride's mother to the first pew on the left just before the wedding begins. She is the last person seated. Although seating the bride's mother is the head usher's responsibility, the bride may elect to have a brother or other family member to have that honor. Please note that for a Jewish ceremony, both of the groom's parents escort him and both of the bride's parents escort her down the aisle and stand with the couple during the ceremony.

After the recessional, the ushers direct the guests out of the church. If the guests do not leave a pathway for the sabre arch team or for the bride and groom to exit, the ushers direct the guests where to stand.

If you decide you don't want a sabre arch or you or your groom is not a commissioned officer, but you want to do something traditional as you exit the chapel, the tradition of throwing rice or birdseed on the departing couple has given way to blowing bubbles (outdoors, of course) as the couple exits the chapel. Remember to pass out the bubbles as the guests are leaving the chapel.

Chaplain vs. Personal Clergy

Although a chaplain adds to the military feel of your military wedding, your wedding and who officiates are very personal matters. To add a personal touch, you may want to ask your pastor, priest, rabbi other clergyperson to officiate, even if the clergyperson is not a military chaplain. However, if you are overseas, using your clergyperson from home (in the States) may not be an option.

Marriage License and Officiant Certification

Even when marrying on a military installation, you and your officiant must still comply with state requirements. If marrying overseas, you should check with your commander for guidance. There may be regulations you must comply with if you, as a military member, plan to marry while assigned overseas.

Guest Books and Receiving Lines

Guest books and receiving lines should be done at the reception rather than at the chapel. Again, many chapels have limits on the amount of time you can use the chapel. These time constraints do not allow enough time for receiving lines or the time necessary for all guests to sign a guest book as they arrive, plus the ceremony and the after-ceremony photo session. Guest book signing and receiving lines can be conducted in a more relaxed setting at the reception.

VIP Guests

If the groom's (or bride's) parents cannot attend the wedding, you may ask your commander and spouse to sit where your parents would sit during the ceremony. Also, if the bride's father, a relative or close friend is unable to be present, the bride's commander or the groom's commander may be given the honor of escorting the bride down the aisle if the commander knows the bride especially well.[9]

If you expect senior military or civilian officials to attend your wedding, you may want to designate special seating for these guests. Consult your local protocol officer for assistance in working out the seating arrangement details. Also, consider appointing one of your ushers, who is familiar with your VIP guests, to be responsible for seating your special guests. If your VIP guests arrive without a personal driver, designating an usher as a VIP parking valet is a nice gesture--a nice touch, but not required.

Chapter 7

Your Reception

The reception for a military wedding is similar to a non-military wedding. A military wedding reception may be held at an officers' club, an enlisted club or any other reception venue. Information from most wedding planning books will give you great guidance. Below are some ideas to consider for a military wedding reception.

Arrival

Allow time for the wedding party to freshen up after they arrive at the reception.

If you have not made specific plans (i.e. sabre arch) for your departure from the chapel, you may direct your guests to the reception to begin the social hour while the wedding party completes the after ceremony photo session.

You may ask an usher, a friend or family member to greet your guests and invite them into the reception area. Your greeter may direct your guests through the receiving line if you decide to have one.[10]

A receiving line is not necessary at small receptions (usually fewer than fifty guests). Guests should congratulate the groom, but not the bride. The bride is wished happiness and complimented on her beauty. (To congratulate the bride implies congratulations on "catching a husband.")

Toasts

The first toasts are done the same as any other wedding. However, after the fathers of the groom and bride propose toasts, the commander of the military member of the newlyweds may offer a toast to the couple.

If both the bride and groom are military, then, the groom's commander, then the bride's commander should propose the toasts regardless of each commander's rank. Wedding etiquette takes precedence in deciding the toasting order. During a wedding reception, the protocol of the wedding sets the order. As with other toasts, the person connected with the groom goes first; then the person connected to the bride. This is a suggested toasting order:

- Best Man
- Maid (or Matron) of Honor (optional)
- Parents of the Groom (optional)
- Parents of the Bride (optional)
- Commander of the Groom (optional)
- Commander of the Bride (optional)
- Relatives (optional)
- Friends (Optional)
- Groom
- Bride

Cake cutting

When it's time to cut the wedding cake, if the groom has a sword, he unsheathes it and hands it to the bride. She holds the sword, the groom places his hand over hers, and together they cut the first piece of cake from the bottom tier. Then, the bride offers the groom the first bite of cake followed by the groom offering the bride the next bite. The bride and groom may feed each other with their fingers or with a fork. The tradition of the bride and groom cutting and sharing the first slice of cake symbolizes their willingness to work together and to share.

If no sabre or sword is available, a silver cake knife may be used, possibly decorated at the handle with ribbon streamers. Also, be sure to have napkins readily available on the cake table.

If using a sabre or sword to cut the cake, please, I repeat, please do not forget to clean the sabre (sword) before placing it back in the sheath (scabbard).[11] The dried sugar residue from the cake may damage the sabre (sword), makes it difficult to remove the sabre (sword) from the sheath (scabbard) and also makes it next to impossible to clean the icing residue in the sheath (scabbard).

Children

Those who are invited and attend should be well behaved. Even at the reception, children should not be allowed to run about freely, nor should they be allowed to join in with the young single adults when they gather and attempt to catch the bride's garter or bouquet.[12]

Decoration

To set a patriotic or military theme for your reception here are a few suggestions:

- Instead of a gift basket or wishing well for gift envelopes, decorate a basket, mailbox, bird cage, box with a patriotic theme

- Include military or patriotic items, ideas or colors in the decorations

- Use the names of places you have visited, been assigned, want to be assigned or where you met instead of the usual table numbers.

- Select wedding favors with a patriotic theme

- Make a donation in the names of your guests to an organization that supports members of the armed forces instead of a traditional wedding favor. Provide a card at each place setting to let your guests know about your gesture. The I Do Foundation, the nation's first wedding-focused nonprofit foundation, may be an ideal way to do this. The I Do Foundation helps couples to raise donations for the charity of their choice.

- Place the U.S. flag, service flag and unit flag behind the receiving line

Chapter 8

Wedding Flowers

If the bride decides to wear her uniform instead of a wedding gown, she may still carry a small, elegant bouquet. Boutonnieres are not allowed on military uniforms. However, any male ceremony participant not in uniform may wear a boutonniere.

There are usually restrictions on decorations at military chapels. Since most are historic buildings or landmarks, you may be prohibited from pinning, taping, tacking, stapling, or attaching decorations in any fashion to the walls or pews. For safety reasons, there may also be restrictions concerning the use of candles (such as candle arch, candelabra, etc.) as decorations.

However, you should talk to your florist on how to be creative about adding decorations. As restrictive as this may seem, it really is not. The challenge is to your imagination, creative talents and the creativity of your florist and wedding coordinator or planner to develop a plan to achieve the look you want within the rules.

Keep in mind that your set up and tear down time is limited. It is advisable for you to stay away from elaborate decorations that take more than 10 to 15 minutes to set up or remove. Most military chapels are beautiful without any added adornment. Too much decoration for a military wedding detracts from the simple elegance of this type of wedding.

Since you must remove your floral arrangements immediately after the ceremony, consider how you can use your ceremony floral arrangements to decorate the reception location. Make sure you designate someone to begin transporting most of the arrangements to the reception location as soon as the guests exit the sanctuary. Also, make plans to transport the remaining flowers to the reception location after the post-ceremony photo session is finished.

Additionally, decide in advance what you want to do with your floral arrangements after the reception. Some ideas are:

- Give the floral arrangements to your parents to use for a brunch the day after the wedding

- Give the floral arrangements to the guests

- Give the floral arrangements to a hospital or nursing home

- Have someone take floral arrangements to sick or elderly relatives who were unable to attend the wedding.

The generosity of the giver always seems to return as a blessing to the giver. Giving away, rather than throwing away, the floral arrangements from your wedding ceremony and reception will usually do wonders to lift someone's spirit. What a nice way to start a marriage.

Chapter 9

Photography, Videography and Publicity

Your photographer and videographer should not move around the area of the altar or chancel until after the ceremony is over. No flash photography during the ceremony. Many historic buildings prohibit flash photography. Once one person uses a flash, everyone with a camera wants to take photographs during the ceremony.

Many officiants will allow only the photographer and videographer contracted by the bride and groom to take pictures or record during the ceremony. The constant flashing of cameras during the ceremony is distracting and, possibly, blinding for the person facing the flashes. Your marriage ceremony is a scared moment. Ask your officiant to announce at the start of the ceremony that there will be no flash photography and ask guests to turn off cell phones. You may also place a note in the ceremony program.

Your photographer and videographer should be unobtrusive and not interfere with the flow of the processional, ceremony or recessional.

Newspaper Announcements

As a military member, you may be assigned far away from your hometown and family. Like many newly engaged and newlywed couples, you want the world to know about this special time in your life. One way to do this is through local and hometown newspaper announcements. Each newspaper has guidelines for accepting engagement and wedding announcements. Three ways to get the submission information for your announcements are:

1. Contact your Public Affairs Office where you are assigned to get contact information for the newspaper you are interested in placing your announcement. Then, contact the newspaper for their submission guidelines.

2. Check the Internet. Most publications have websites. The submission criteria for placing an engagement or wedding announcement may be included.

3. Ask a friend from your hometown to assist you. The friend may be more than happy to help you as a way to join in the celebration of your wedding, even if they are unable to attend your long distance wedding location.

Chapter 10

Wedding Gifts

Gift registry! Gift registry! Gift registry! Guests should be advised to send wedding gifts to your home before or after the wedding. If you will be moving shortly after the wedding, your guests should be encouraged to send gifts to you at your new duty station after the wedding. Gift registries make this easy for you and the people you invite to your wedding. Some registries may hold the gifts until you are ready to pick up the gifts or have them delivered.

Although receiving a wedding invitation implies an obligation to give a gift. The obligation is implied. To place gift registry information or a "no gifts" statement in your invitation makes a gift the expected admission price to attend your wedding. This is offensive and in poor taste.

Please encourage your guests not to bring wedding gifts to the wedding or reception. Although it has been a long-standing practice, it is actually an etiquette *faux pas*. Refraining from bringing gifts to the wedding and reception is a considerate gesture. After a full day of festivities the newlyweds, parents, other family members and friends do not have to worry about how the gifts are going to get home or how the gifts are going to be shipped to your new home.

If you are in the process of being reassigned, the military may arrange to ship your gifts as part of your household shipment. Check with your transportation management office for the most current information and the best advice.

Chapter 11

Unexpected Situations

Wedding Insurance

Due to the possibility of short notice military reassignments and deployment, you may want to consider WedSafe wedding insurance. Wedding insurance is a specialty insurance package with clearly defined sections that provide financial protection for certain types of potential losses (e.g., postponement, theft of rings or presents, damage to dresses or wedding attire, and loss of deposits), during the period leading up to and including your wedding day.

The WedSafe wedding insurance policy will provide coverage if the bride or groom is serving in the armed forces, police department or fire department and must postpone the wedding and or reception due to a previously granted leave being withdrawn due to circumstances beyond their control (e.g., unforeseen deployment or state of emergency).

Policy premiums are one-time only payments. The policy can be purchased by completing the simple application form available online at www.wedsafe.com or by calling a WedSafe wedding insurance policy representative toll free at (877) 723-3933.[13]

Increased Alert Status or Elevated Threat Advisories

The normal force protection condition for a military post or base is A or Alpha. The threat of attack is low. This level is similar to a Department of Homeland Security "Low" or "Guarded" threat advisory. To ensure all of your guests and vendors will be able to gain access, call Base Security or the Provost Marshall to find out what type of information you will need to provide to make entering the base or post easier.

A list of your guests and vendors may be required. Include your entire list of invitees, not just the ones who reply for your reception. This is in case you have someone who can make the wedding ceremony and not the reception and doesn't have a military identification card. Also, include guests and vendors who may have a military identification card. What if you think they do have an identification card and they don't? It is usually easy for your non-military guests and vendors to gain access under condition Alpha.

However, if the force protection condition, alert status or the Department of Homeland Security threat advisory is elevated for any reason, expect gaining access to be a bit more difficult and time consuming. Expect a 100 percent identification check. Even expect a random car search (under the car chassis with mirrors, under the hood, inside the car, inside the trunk). This applies to private as well as commercial vehicles, including limousines.

Also, be aware that the military police may make a random search of a vehicle even under force protection condition Alpha. Remember, this is for the protection of the military installation and those who live, work or are visiting. How can they do this search? You give implied consent to be searched when you try to gain access to the installation.

You should give your family, wedding party, expected guests and vendors some special instructions when the force protection condition is Alpha (A), Bravo (B) or Charlie (C):

1. Arrive at least one hour early to get through the identification check and car search at the gate. The line may be long. Also, the installation may require you to be shuttled to the chapel or club instead of using your own car or hired limousine. You want to allow plenty of time so you don't miss your own wedding. I have seen guests, who did not heed the warning, miss all, but the last 15 to 30 minutes of an hour long Nuptial Mass. If it had been a 30 to 45 minute Protestant ceremony, they would have missed the entire ceremony.

2. Be sure to have identification. A military identification card, driver's license or other government issued or civilian employment photo identification card should suffice. This also applies to the bride and her wedding party.

3. Bring the wedding invitation. Although it's not required, it is additional evidence of why you are trying to gain access to the installation and where you are headed.

4. Do not give the military police a difficult time. Remember, even though your guest's name is on your list, the police don't have to give them entry if they think your guest poses a threat. Also, remember, the police are carrying loaded weapons.

5. Do not attempt to bring a weapon onto a military installation. If members of your wedding party, family members or guests are law enforcement officers, contact base Security or Provost Marshall for the procedure to bring their weapons onto the installation.

These tips apply for the rehearsal, ceremony and reception. These also apply to the bride and groom. If you don't arrive in time for your wedding, don't expect to get married at the chapel. There may be another wedding immediately following your scheduled time. Out of courtesy they should not be bumped because they arrived on time and you did not. This can happen if the chapel is popular for weddings. There could be a full schedule of weddings without a break. I know this sounds harsh. But, would you want someone to bump you out of your scheduled wedding time? Probably not.

Also, to help make gaining access smoother and less time consuming, carpool as much as possible. Then, there will be fewer cars at the gate. Find out which gates are open and provide maps of alternate routes for your guests.

If you have hired a military sabre team for your wedding, you should contact the team leader to be sure they will be able to support your wedding during an increased alert status. The members of the sabre team may not be available because of mission requirements. You may want to have military friends ready to perform the arch as a back-up team, if possible.

One last note, if the force protection condition is Delta (D) or the Department of Homeland Security threat advisory is "Severe," don't expect to gain access to a military installation for your wedding. It means that the area, maybe even the installation, is under attack (i.e. military installations in the Washington, DC metropolitan area on September 11, 2001, now known as 9/11). Only military members and mission essential personnel will be allowed access. Besides, you probably won't want to leave the house. Your groom or bride may not be available. Needless to say, it's not the kind of Star Spangled Banner (rockets red glare and bombs bursting in air) wedding memories most people would want.

Short Notice Reassignment or Deployment

Your fiancé is notified that he (or she) will be leaving in less than 90 days and you don't know if he (or she) can return for your wedding. What do you do?

1. Move up the wedding date. If you can arrange for a sooner wedding date at the chapel, support from your vendors and mail out invitations, you can get married and have the ceremony you have planned before he (or she) departs.

2. Have a private ceremony and plan a later affirmation ceremony and reception similar to your original wedding plans.

3. Or, cancel your wedding and reschedule.

Chapter 12

Post Wedding Concerns

You are married now...The wedding festivities are over...Now, it's time to enter the real world of the military spouse...The adventure begins...What do I do now?

There is no magic impartation of military spouse knowledge and wisdom. If you have never been exposed to military life, you may feel that you have entered a new dimension. I asked friends, who were military spouses, "What would have made your introduction to military life easier?" Some of the answers were: 1) an understanding of the military's mission; 2) why are people reassigned; 3) what is the commissary and the exchange; 4) what do different acronyms mean; 5) how will moving around with the military affect my career?

Attempting to answer all of your questions about military life in this one book is impossible and would be out-of-date by the time this book is released. So, let's start with giving you a few resources to help you navigate military life.

Identification card

If you or your spouse does not have a military identification card, be sure to get your military identification card as soon as possible after you return from your honeymoon. If your honeymoon is delayed, get the card as soon as possible after the wedding.

If you are an active duty member and plan to change your name, be sure to complete the appropriate forms to change your name, and get your new identification card.

If you have a dependent identification card because of your parents, you need to get a new identification card with your new husband or wife as your sponsor.

Moving to the duty station

Be sure to check with your commander about adding your new spouse to your military orders if you are being reassigned.

Also, you may require permission for your spouse to accompany you on an overseas assignment. To prevent disappointment and heartache, do this well in advance so that you and your new spouse are well aware of any special requirements, especially in case a temporary separation is necessary.

Resources

When my friends became military spouses over 20 years ago, there was little or no information available. Today, there are many resources, especially on the Internet, to answer the new military spouse's questions. Here are a few websites to check out:

Military One Source www.militaryonesource.com or 1-800-342-9647

Military OneSource provides you with information and resources that can help improve many areas of your life, from personal to professional. Military One Source does more than give you information -- they help you take action, with materials that get you thinking and tools that help you set things in motion. The service is confidential and available 24 hours a day/7 days a week.

Military Spouse Resource Center www.milspouse.org

The Military Spouse Resource Center is designed to assist the spouses of military members, active duty, reserve and guard. The MilSpouse.org web site is jointly sponsored by the Department of Defense and the Department of Labor.

Their mission is to provide easy access to information, resources, and opportunities related to education, training, and employment within the United States. MilSpouse.org extends services to military spouses directly through this site, through partnerships with other organizations, installation family service centers and the U.S. Department of Labor's local One-Stop Career Centers.

TRICARE www.tricare.osd.mil

TRICARE is the department of Defense's worldwide health care program for active duty and retired uniformed services members and their families. TRICARE consists of TRICARE Prime, a managed care option; TRICARE Extra, a preferred provider option; and TRICARE Standard, a fee-for- service option. TRICARE For Life is also available for Medicare-eligible beneficiaries age 65 and over.

Military Homefront www.militaryhomefront.dod.mil

Military Homefront is the official Department of Defense website for reliable information to help troops and their families, leaders and service providers.

National Military Family Association (NMFA) www.nmfa.org

NMFA's mission is to educate military families concerning their rights, benefits and services available. They also promote and protect the interests of military families by influencing the development and implementation of legislation and policies affecting miltary family and to inform them regarding the issues that affect their lives.

Standardized Topic Exchange Service (SITES) Database

SITES (www.dmdc.osd.mil/appj/sites/login) contains resources for everyone who is relocating from one duty station to another, as well as those working or living on or near an installation. SITES information is posted and kept current by Relocation Assistance Program staff located in family, community, or work-life centers on installations located around the world.

The adventure begins

Welcome to the military family! Reassignments, finances, around-the-clock work schedules, deployments and emotions will attempt to play havoc on your marriage.

First, be sure that you sincerely love your spouse, have a mature, trusting relationship and you are prepared and ready for marriage. There will be challenges that will test the strength of your marriage commitment.

Second, be adaptable and ready to face any challenges.

Third, one day you will look back and laugh about some of your military life adventures and misadventures.

Fourth, love covers a multitude of faults.

Fifth, remember why you married your spouse. I hope it was for love—don't confuse it with lust, which is a potential recipe for heartache, disappointment, disaster and divorce.

Finally, remind yourself regularly about what true love is. Remember, love is an action, a choice and a decision. Whether you are religious or not, the best description I've found for what true love is can be found in the Holy Bible—1 Corinthians 13: 4-8a (NIV):

"Love is patient, love is kind.
It does not envy, it does not boast, it is not proud.
It is not rude, it is not self-seeking, it is not easily angered,
it keeps no record of wrongs.
Love does not delight in evil but rejoices with the truth.
It always protects, always trusts, always hopes, always perseveres.
Love never fails."

In closing, may your marriage be blessed! Make the most of your military adventure!

BIBLIOGRAPHY

Cole, Harriet. Jumping the Broom. Henry Holt and Company. New York. 1993.

Crossley, Anne and Keller, Carol A. The Air Force Wife Handbook: A Complete Social Guide. ABI Press. Sarasota, Florida. 1992.

Crossley, Anne and Keller, Carol A. The Army Wife Handbook: Update and Expanded Second Edition. ABI Press. Sarasota, Florida. 1993.

Gross, Mary Preston and Tomlinson, Mickey. Military Weddings and the Military Ball. Beau Lac Publishers. Chuluota, Florida. 1974.

Swartz, Oretha D. Service Etiquette. Naval Institute Press. Annapolis, Maryland. 1988.

Morin, Laura. *The Everything Wedding Organizer*. Adams Media Corporation. Holbrook, Massachusetts. 1998.

Post, Elizabeth L. Emily Post's Complete Book of Wedding Etiquette (Revised Edition).

Bride's Book of Etiquette

Wedding Insurance 101 presented by the Knot.

www.wedsafe.com Website

Department of Homeland Security

Threat Advisory www.dhs.gov

I Do Foundation www.idofoundation.org

United States Air Force Academy www.usafa.af.mil/hc/weddings

United States Naval Academy www.usna.edu/Chaplains/weddings.htm

United States Military Academy www.usma.edu

United States Coast Guard Academy www.cga.edu/campus/crp/crp.htm

United State Merchant Marine Academy www.usmma.edu/chapel/weddings.htm

End Notes

[1] Cole, Harriet. <u>Jumping the Broom</u>.

[2] Crossley, Alice.

[3] Gross, M.P. and Tomlinson, M. <u>Military Weddings and the Military Ball</u>.

[4] Gross, M.P. and Tomlinson, M. <u>Military Weddings and the Military Ball</u>.

[3] Crossley. Wives Handbook

[8] Crossley. Wives Handbook.

[9] Gross, M.P. and Tomlinson, M. <u>Military Weddings and the Military Ball</u>.

[10] Crossley.

[11] Crossley

[12] Crossley

[13] www.wedsafe.com

About the Author

Vanessa L. Baldwin is the President of Elegant Beginnings, a wedding consulting and planning service in Northern Virginia.

Ms. Baldwin is a graduate of University of Maryland Baltimore County and Howard University School of Social Work, Washington, DC.

After professional experience as a social caseworker and a social science analyst, Ms. Baldwin was commissioned as an officer in the United States Air Force. Ms. Baldwin retired from the Air Force in 1998.

The Association of Certified Wedding Consultants, Plano, Texas, certified Ms. Baldwin as a wedding consultant in 1997. Then, she established Elegant Beginnings, providing a full range of wedding planning services in the Metropolitan DC and Northern Virginia areas. Ms. Baldwin specializes in, but is not limited to, military weddings.

In 2004, Ms. Baldwin developed the Wedding Coordinator Certificate Program to train wedding planning professionals. Ms. Baldwin began teaching the first series of courses at the Northern Virginia Community College, Woodbridge Campus in the Fall of 2004.

Ms. Baldwin resides in Woodbridge, Virginia.

www.ingramcontent.com/pod-product-compliance
Lightning Source LLC
Chambersburg PA
CBHW021248280526
45784CB00005B/2286